The Riverside County Chronicles

A Journal of the History of
Riverside County, California

Published by the
Riverside County Heritage Association

For subscription information, along with publication and
submission parameters, please visit our web site:
www.riversidecountyheritageassociation.org

Issue No. 28   Spring 2023

In this Issue

Welcome to the 28th edition of the Riverside County Chronicles! We are so fortunate to be able to put out our publication. While we hope that you continue to enjoy this journal dedicated to the history of Riverside County and will encourage others to subscribe and contribute, please understand that it is difficult to keep offering this without input from you the readers. We need people to step up and contribute - that's the only way we will keep going!

We begin this issue on a sad note. Not one but two eulogies are being printed here, both of which are for major players in local history in their respective areas. The first is for Darell Farnbach. Darell was a stalwart supporter of Temecula's history and, together with his wife Rebecca, were instrumental in getting the County of Riverside and a developer to see the worth in the old Wolf Store/Vail Ranch Headquarters. Through their work, that site was restored and is now a major focus of attention in eastern Temecula.

Next is Ruth Atkins' memorial. Ruth was a wonderful asset to Lake Elsinore, its museum, and its history. She was a staunch supporter of both this journal and the Riverside County History Symposium, and to the greater Lake Elsinore community at large. The passing of these two people leave a large hole in local history that will be difficult if not impossible to fill.

Fortunately, we've able to put together some great articles in this edition too! We start with Virginia Searl Sisk who enlightens us about the Searl Ranch in Diamond Valley. As you may be able to guess, Virginia is a member of that family and gives us a unique perspective into this large farming operation that was in the area for nearly a century.

Next, stalwart Moreno Valley researcher Deanna La Cava tells us the story of Rosa Lyman More, one of the pioneers of that region. Deanna gives us a great insight into the trials and tribulations that Rosa went through as she helped to bring about early Moreno Valley.

Finally, we are honored to have John Brown of the law firm of Best, Best & Krieger join us. John has been revamping the firm's long and storied history, and brings us an article detailing the early years of that firm and its major players. It's a fascinating look into the background of a Riverside firm that is very well known.

Thank you for your continued support of local history in Riverside County. We at the Riverside County Heritage Association enjoy bringing this journal to you in May and November of each year. If you know of anyone who would be interested in either contributing articles or subscribing, please put them in touch with us - we'd love to have more of both!

Steve Lech, President
Riverside County Heritage Association

The Riverside County Chronicles

Table of Contents

In Memoriam: Darell Farnbach 　*by Rebecca Farnbach*	4
In Memoriam: Ruth Atkins 　*by Kim McElroy*	8
The Searl Ranch: A Diamond Valley Farming Operation 　from 1893 to 1989 　*by Virginia Searl Sisk*	10
Postcards From Our Area	17
Rosa Lyman More, Moreno Valley Pioneer 　*by Deanna La Cava*	18
An Early History of the Law Firm of Best, Best & Krieger LLP 　*by John Brown et al*	22
About the Authors	33

In Memoriam

Darell Farnbach

Founding member, Vail Ranch Restoration Association
Stalwart champion of the history of Temecula and the region
Perpetual volunteer, collector, "go-to" guy

Darell Farnbach
April 14, 1942 - March 14, 2023

Darell Farnbach was a fourth generation Californian who lived in the mountains, in the desert, and in the city in this state. He experienced life in California from as far south as Temecula and to near the northern border in Alturas.

The story of Darell Joe Farnbach begins when the two men who would become his grandfathers began working on the Red Line in Los Angeles in the early 1900s. Albert Cash, who was a New Englander from Nantucket Island and worked as a motorman on the Red Line, began to homestead some land in the San Gabriel Mountains near Wrightwood, California in 1916, but found it was too much work for him. He offered to split the land with his coworker Joe Farnbach, a first-generation German born in America who was a conductor on the Red Line, if he would help him with the mandatory improvements on the homestead.

The teamwork made the two families grow close. After their children Alberta Cash and Gerald Farnbach met as children, their friendship grew into love. Gerald and Alberta attended Life Bible College in Los Angeles, founded by the famous female evangelist Aimee Semple McPherson. They were joined in marriage in 1929 in a double wedding ceremony performed by McPherson.

Three children were born to Gerald and Alberta, with Darell coming last at White Memorial Hospital in Los Angeles on April 14, 1942. For a while the family lived in Los Angeles and then they moved to the family homestead, the rustic Wrightwood Lazy B-J-F Ranch.

After a while, the Farnbachs' marriage dissolved and Darell went to live with his father, stepmother, and stepsiblings Sheila and David Brooks in Ukiah, California where they soon welcomed Darell's baby brother Bob. Later, Darell lived with his Grandmother and Grandfather Farnbach in Auburn, California.

Darell wanted to live with his mother, and after some persuasion, he got his way. He lived with her on the Lockhart Ranch near Barstow, where she was a cook. His mother eventually married a cowboy named Cliff Johnson who gave Darell an extended family with aunts and uncles and cousins.

Darell moved with Cliff and Alberta to Kelsey, in the Placerville area, where Cliff worked for the Forest Service. Some of their adventures in Kelsey included building a cabin and an outhouse, interacting with odd neighbors, and attending a two-room school where Darell was valedictorian of a class of three students.

After a few years the family moved to Alturas on Highway 395 at the Oregon border and then before Darell's senior year of high school they moved to Monrovia where Darell graduated in 1960.

Having an income was always important to Darell. Trying to earn some spending money, Darell bought 100 baby chicks when he was twelve years old. He raised them and sold them dressed and afterward did not ever want to raise chickens again.

Darell always loved cars. He started driving when he was about six years old. He drove a Model A to the end of their long country lane where he and his brother and sister caught the school bus. Darell would stand on the seat to steer while his brother worked the pedals. Also, as a child he would drive across the desert while his stepdad and uncle lay on the running boards shooting rabbits.

Darell's first job was washing cars for an auto sales agency. He remembers the thrill of driving the cars that he washed. In Monrovia he worked in a convalescent hospital, a pharmacy, and a gas station. He considered going into mortuary science but decided instead to attend beauty college.

He excelled as a hair stylist and earned credentials to teach at the beauty school. It was there that he met his first wife, Ramona Rubio. They married in 1965. Darell was drafted into the Army in 1966 and was a battery clerk stationed in Schweinfurt, Germany, where their daughter Darya was born. After returning to California, Darell purchased a salon in Arcadia and son Todd was born in 1971.

In 1981 the family moved to Temecula where Darell and Ramona formed the Farnbach Aldstadt Design Company with another couple from the Arcadia area. They did commercial and residential interior design in the fast-growing area, while Darell continued traveling to Arcadia every other week to work in his salon.

Darell also collected and restored antiques and had an antique store inside the Temecula Mercantile building.

When Darell's and Ramona's marriage ended, an Arcadia hair client introduced Darell to Rebecca. They married seven months later and Darell persuaded Rebecca to move to Temecula. Darell helped her to raise her teenage children Andrew and Abigail Marshall.

Anyone who knew Darell knows he loved cars. Until recently he had a Model A pickup, a Model T roadster, a 1938 Cadillac LaSalle, and 1970 and 1972 Ford Mustang convertibles. Before he moved to Temecula, he owned two of his favorite cars, a Packard convertible and a Mercedes convertible. His salon in Temecula "The Pink Caddy" featured the front clip of a 1969 Fleetwood Cadillac as the reception desk. He owned about 70 cars during his lifetime.

Through the years Darell became a close friend to others who enjoyed classic cars, most notably the Drifters Car Club members. A highpoint in Darell's life was going with some of the Drifters to drive exotic cars onto the auction block for Mecum Auto Auctions. In 2019 Darell's red 1972 Mustang Convertible was featured in Mustang Monthly magazine.

When Darell and Rebecca became empty nesters, they began to advocate for the Vail Headquarters historic site that was threatened with demolition. Darell was a plaintiff in the suit that settled favorably. Darell spent many hours each week overseeing the restoration, as well as setting up a small museum called the Little Temecula History Center with others in the Vail Ranch Restoration Association.

Darell's faith in God was a guiding force in his life. When Darell was about six years old, he responded to an altar call at a Nazarene Church he attended with his Grandma Farnbach. His heart and behavior were changed after he asked Jesus to come into his life and he never forgot what a difference knowing Christ made in him. Darell specified that old hymns including The Old Rugged Cross be sung at his memorial gathering.

The Temecula Chamber of Commerce named the Farnbachs the 2019 Citizen of the Year and in 2021 their names were placed on the Wall of Honor in the Temecula City Hall.

Darell passed away at home on March 14 at in Temecula, California after a long illness. His brother Garry Farnbach preceded him in death. Darell is survived by his wife Rebecca, sister Donna Reese of Bishop, California, brother Robert Farnbach of Ukiah, California, and stepsiblings Sheila Brooks of Ukiah, California, and David Brooks of Sacramento, California. He leaves children Todd of Medford, Oregon, Darya of Fairhaven, Vermont, and their spouses, stepson Andrew Marshall of Temecula, California, stepdaughter Abigail Juarez and her husband of Wildomar, California, grandchildren Terran and Taj Farnbach, and Natalia Kartaszynska, five step-grandchildren, and many nephews and nieces.

Darell loved Temecula and was proud to have been part of the restoration of Vail Headquarters, but he said his best legacy was his children, which included his stepchildren and grandchildren. He was loved by many in the community and will be long remembered, especially by the third-grade students who took bumpy rides in Darell's Model A at Vail Headquarters during field trips.

In Memoriam

Ruth Atkins

President Emeritus, Lake Elsinore Historical Society
Long-time Riverside County Historical Commission member
Champion of all things Lake Elsinore, especially its history
Gracious donor
Perpetual volunteer

Ruth Atkins
November 22, 1931 - December 2, 2022

Ruth Atkins will be remembered as a woman of great kindness and integrity. She was a mentor and a community leader, a historian and a political activist. She is described by colleagues as "feisty" and by dear friends as "stubborn." One of her dearest friends shared that if ever a road was to be named after her, "it would need to be called Atkins' Way." If she decided to do something she was all in until it was done to her satisfaction.

Ruth moved to Lake Elsinore in 1994 but did not become active in the city until the death of her husband. Within a short time she realized she would have to find something that would engage her and give her something to do. "My derriere doesn't fit a rocking chair," she once stated. In 1997, Donna Morin, founder of the Lake Elsinore Historical Society heard about her through mutual friends and invited her to a meeting. By the end of this meeting, she had accepted the role of secretary to the organization and quickly set to work helping the museum grow and learning all she could about the history of the area. Within a few years she took on the role of treasurer and in 2007 she became the president of the organization, a position she continued to hold until 2021 when she stepped into the role of President Emeritus to mentor her successor.

Several years ago, Ruth was named to the Riverside County Historical Commission. She took on numerous projects to save and preserve important parts of the area's history. In 1999 she assisted in the efforts to restore the 1925 American LaFrance fire truck that had been put in storage since the 1960's. Another restoration project Ruth actively supported was the restoration of the Barkschat Marbelite Lamp Posts that again line Lake Shore Drive. She, along with others from LEHS, encouraged the city to restore the Mary McDonald Gazebo and drinking fountain on Heald Street in the city and was instrumental in making it a historic landmark in the town. She learned that Lake Elsinore had a WWI cargo ship named after it and worked with Rick Reiss to research the ship while she commissioned a miniature model to be built of it. These are just a few of her many accomplishments during her time in Lake Elsinore.

Ruth received many honors, most recently, she received the 67th Assembly District Woman of the Year of 2022 in the last year of her life.

Ruth will be missed by many and treasured by everyone who knew her. As a researcher, historian, political activist and mentor to many, Ruth was a valuable resource in Lake Elsinore. Her friends will tell you they will miss her quick wit and piercing blue eyes. Her sharp mind and strong will provided the strength and guidance needed to make a difference. Well-loved and well-respected by everyone, she remained a humble woman with a passion to serve. She was a powerful force in our town and leaves us with a greater awareness of our past. She was a powerful force in our town. Her passion for Lake Elsinore and the surrounding region was well-known, as was her commitment to the history of the region.

The Searl Ranch:

A Diamond Valley Farming Operation from 1893 to 1989

By Virginia Searl Sisk

One of Riverside County's landmarks is Diamond Valley Lake, southwest of Hemet. Long before water filled this manmade lake, early settlers established farms and homes. This article traces the family history of Oliver and Idella Searl, the author's ancestors who first settled into Diamond Valley in the 1890s.

Oliver Cromwell Searl was born in 1849 in Somanauk, Illinois. His family traveled west and settled in Watsonville, California. After Oliver's parents relocated in his teens, he began traveling around Southern California with his older brothers. His early adult years were spent working as a teamster hauling borax out of Death Valley with a 20-mule team. He lived and worked in San Diego in the 1880s, sold his property there, then moved to Winchester (before the formation of Riverside County).

Meanwhile, Amanda Wisdom, the seventh child of David and Sarah Wisdom, of Urbana, Missouri, was born February 3, 1854. As a teenager in the early 1870s, Amanda moved to Springfield, Missouri, and married a man by the last name of Hutton. Amanda gave birth to Idella Florence Hutton on July 14, 1874, at age 20. Mr. Hutton left Amanda after Idella's birth, and nothing else is known about Hutton, including his first name.

Amanda, with baby Idella, returned to her parents in Urbana, Missouri. Amanda then married Thomas J. Reinhart. Later, the Reinhart family moved west, where the weather was milder, due to Amanda's severe asthma. In 1888, they traveled via the Santa Fe Railroad to their destination of San Jacinto. By that year, Idella had many half-brothers and half-sisters from the Reinhart parents.

Thomas Reinhart established his government claim in what is now known as Reinhart Canyon, west of Hemet. Thomas and Amanda settled down in their new homestead, with their large brood of children, of which Idella was the oldest (and by then, went by Idella Reinhart). Idella later remembered a carved, decorated Indian rock in Reinhart Canyon, on which she played as a child.

Sometime between 1888 and 1891, Idella and Oliver met in the Winchester area (Reinhart Canyon is three miles north of Winchester). After a courtship, they were married at the Winchester Methodist Church in 1892, when Oliver was 37 and Idella was 17. Idella later told those who would listen that being the oldest girl in a large family left her with many babysitting duties while her parents worked all day. Apparently,

Idella and Oliver's first house in Diamond Valley.

she was eager to avoid the constant babysitting of younger siblings.

Oliver and Idella rented a two-room house in Winchester until June of 1893, when their first-born son, Edgar, was a year old. They searched for land to buy, and even looked as far away as Corona, but thought it was too far from Idella's family. They finally bought 25 acres in Diamond Valley. That 25 acres was the beginning of the Searl ranching era. The nearby town of Hemet had not yet been incorporated.

Idella and Oliver Searl had nine children: Edgar, Harry, Garner, Gerald, Ethel, Clyde, Floyd, Evelyn, and Edna. Piece by piece, Oliver and Idella increased the size of their farm by buying neighboring acreages as they came up for sale. All the children worked on the ranch and attended Diamond Valley's one-room schoolhouse. This was the only school in the tiny Diamond Valley District.

During harvest season, "Mother Searl" cooked for the farm crews at the farmhouse. When the crews worked too far afield, she traveled to them in a covered wagon, in which was mounted a wood-burning stove. Mother Searl prepared meals for the working men until ill health forced her to curtail such work in her later years.

In 1915 Oliver Searl purchased a Holt Combine to harvest the grain. The huge harvester was drawn by twenty or more horses and mules. As the huge center wheels turned, the grain thresher blades cut and separated the wheat. Workers gathered the grain and put it into gunny sacks in a room at the top of the harvester. They sewed each sack closed with nine stitches. Horse-drawn wagons carried the full sacks to the ranch.

Oliver's health failed and he died in 1921. Three of his older sons, Edgar, Harry, and Gerald, managed the

Twelve year old Harry Searl and his team taking 100-pound sacks of barley from a Diamond Valley field in 1906 to the Hemet Train Depot. Thirty years later, Harry was elected mayor of Hemet and served eight years in that role. He played a crucial role in establishing Hemet's first community hospital.

A hired hand steadies the mule while Oliver and his six sons clown around.

business. The three brothers transformed the family farm into a commercially viable enterprise. The abundance of grain gave them enough to feed their pigs and horses, and to sell enough grain to purchase more land. In addition to their Diamond Valley acreage, they leased the Wolfskill Ranch in Moreno Valley from 1921-1984. They were then able to grow even more wheat, barley, and oats to sell. In Diamond Valley, the brothers eventually opened a cattle feedlot, which replaced the raising of pigs.

The Searl Cattle Feedlot

Cattle feed was prepared in a mill on the ranch. The food consisted of oats, barley, alfalfa, and molasses (which was added to the mixture to make the food more palatable for the cows). The author's father, Floyd, would drive a truck carrying a big tank to Long Beach, where the tank would be filled with molasses before returning to the ranch. The cattle feed was then loaded into a large feeding truck and taken to the cattle pens. In the early years of cattle raising, calves were brought into Hemet and driven (walking, not in a truck) down State Street and then over to the cattle pens.

This author's parents, Floyd Searl and his bride, Claire Gilman, from Banning, began their married life on the Wolfskill Ranch in Moreno in 1928. They lived there for ten years until 1938, when they moved to Hemet so their daughter, Virginia, would have a place to go to school. At that time, there were no schools in that part of Moreno Valley.

By 1931, huge tractors replaced horses and mules pulling the harvesters. At the beginning of World War II, the grain was handled in bulk. Searl

(Above) A powerful tractor pulls the harvester on the leased Moreno Ranch.

(Below) Truck being emptied of its grain to be augered up into a grain bin.

grandchildren would drive trucks out to the harvesters and load up grain. They drove the loaded grain trucks back to the ranch and maneuvered up on a loading platform, where the grain augered up into grain bins.

In 1932, the three brothers legally formed the Searl Brothers partnership. In 1944, Floyd, the youngest brother, also became a partner. The ranch prospered and grew, so much that, in the 1960s, more than 8,000 acres of grain were being planted and harvested each year on a combination of Diamond Valley land and the Moreno Wolfskill Ranch.

In the early decades of Searl Diamond Valley operations, the only farming possible was dry land farming. In 1954, Eastern Municipal Water District began to pipe water to Diamond Valley. Tracks of land that had been committed to dryland farming of grain could then be irrigated. The Searl Brothers partnership quickly converted some crops using irrigation water. While still dry-farming large acreages of grain, their main irrigated crops were potatoes, alfalfa, and watermelons.

With the death of Ed, Harry, and Gerald in the 1960's, the Searl Brothers partnership was superseded by Searl Farms. The principals of this new entity were Floyd, the surviving brother, Leonard Searl (the son of Edgar), and Jerry Searl (the son of Gerald). Floyd retired in 1971 and Jerry died in 1985, leaving Leonard as the last Searl to actively manage the ranch.

In 1989, Metropolitan Water District WD bought the Searl Ranch to become part of a water storage facility that would serve the needs of a large portion of Southern California in times of drought or other emergencies. All of the homes, barns, silos, corrals, and other buildings and fixtures that made up the Searl Ranch were razed, and the farmland today lies at the bottom of Diamond Valley Lake.

Idella worked her garden to feed both her family and the farm workers

Diamond Valley Lake today

Postcards From Our Area

*Two views of downtowns in early Riverside County.
Above, Main Street in Palm Springs circa 1930.
Below, "the highway" through Murrieta, circa 1915.
Both postcards from the collection of Steve Lech.*

Rosa Lyman More

Moreno Valley Pioneer

by Deanna La Cava

Rosa Lyman More was a true pioneer hailing from a family of pioneers. Rosa's grandfather, Amasa Lyman, led a wagon train that arrived in San Bernardino from Utah in 1851. Grandpa Lyman and Charles C. Rich were appointed by Brigham Young, a leader of the Church of Jesus Christ of Latter-day Saints, to establish a colony in San Bernardino, California.

Leading 100 families from Salt Lake City, it took the train of approximately 500 people three months to finally arrive at Sycamore Grove, at the mouth of the Cajon Pass near today's Glen Helen Parkway. An entry in the diary of Mary Phelps Rich, a wife of Charles Rich, describes, "Finally arrived at what was called Cajon Pass. From here we went down into the valley beyond. We camped in several different places, about a half a mile apart, so to give our cattle plenty of ground. Here, too, we held religious services. When we reached the place where it was intended we should settle, we found things ready for us as Mr. Rich and Mr. Lyman had gone ahead to arrange for our comfort. They had staked out places to camp. These were in a Sycamore grove."

The pioneers camped at Sycamore Grove for three months while Lyman and Rich negotiated a deal to purchase Rancho San Bernardino from the Lugo family. During this layover, Rosa's father, Lorenzo Snow Lyman, was born on November 6, 1851. According to a 1938 article in the San Bernardino Daily Sun, Lorenzo Snow Lyman has the distinction of being the first white child born in the San Bernardino valley. Ultimately, Amasa Lyman and Charles Rich purchased 35,000 acres from the Lugos for $77,500. The Mormon colonists founded the settlement of San Bernardino and built the Fort at San Bernardino. In 1857, Brigham Young recalled the faithful back to Utah so the Lyman family, with 6-year-old Lorenzo, took the long and dangerous overland journey back to Utah.

At the age of 24, Lorenzo, now with his young wife, Zuriah Rowley, made the journey overland by team and wagon back to California and began farming in Santa Barbara. It was here that Rosa Lyman, their third child, was born on December 7, 1878.

In 1888, Lorenzo Lyman moved his family by covered wagon to the Alessandro valley to take up a homestead claim on a quarter section along Kitching Street and Kalmia Avenue, a mile north of what is today Highway 60. In an interview with Weezy Wold for the "Press Enterprise" in 1970, Rosa told of moving here when she was nine years old. "I remember my mother and what a time she must have had caring for five children. I remember the wagon

(Above) The New Settlers
The headquarters and stables of the Alessandro Orange Grove and Fruit Company at the height of its development. The company incorporated in 1890 planting an orchard of 700 acres in the spring of 1891 with 500 acres in oranges, 100 in prunes, 90 in peaches, and 10 in apricots (Photo courtesy of the Moreno Valley Historical Society).

(Below) Large acreages were planted in 1891 but water stopped flowing to Moreno. Fruit trees were cut up and used for firewood. By 1895 the personal property of the fruit company was being sold at auction. The valley reverted to desert when the water was withdrawn (Photo courtesy of the Moreno Valley Historical Society).

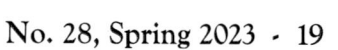

Opening in 1893 with 20 students, Cloverdale School was located on the southwest corner of Ironwood Avenue and Judson Street (today's Perris Boulevard). The school was described as a fine, big building with high ceilings, one large classroom, beautiful woodwork, wardrobes, anterooms and a big steeple on one corner that held a bell. After about a dozen years, attendance was so low Cloverdale School closed, and students began attending the original Midland School at Alessandro Boulevard and Kitching Street. This photo was taken about 1896 (Photo courtesy of the Moreno Valley Historical Society).

stopping and the bread she cooked over an open fire."

At the time, the only settlement in the valley was the tiny ghost town of Alessandro located about where Van Buren Boulevard now ends at the I-215 freeway. The town of Alessandro had only four buildings: a railroad station, a post office, a vacant store building, and a hotel. In a 1955 Butterfield Express interview, Rosa commented, "I don't know when the hotel was built or why, but when we came to the Valley, it was being used as a residence by Mr. and Mrs. W. F. Warner and their five children. There were only four other families here then. Their dry land farms where they raised barley, wheat and oats were scattered. The Lorenzo Lyman family, a second Lyman family [cousins of Lorenzo], and the Van Leuvens had farms at the base of the mountain range near a source of spring water. The Sanders lived in Box Springs canyon.

The former store at Alessandro was converted into a schoolhouse for the 17 children of the settlers. Their teacher, Miss Angie Farnsworth, boarded with the Warners. In reminiscing about the valley back in 1888, Rosa said, "The land was barren, a desert. Coyotes roamed freely and when we drove to school, we often saw herds of antelope."

Around 1890, a change came to the area as the Bear Valley and Alessandro Development Company piped water from Bear Valley, over the Redlands grade and into Moreno. With the coming of irrigation, hundreds of families poured into the valley. Vineyards, orchards, and orange groves suddenly appeared, and Moreno Valley became prosperous.

The new settlers petitioned to form a school district. The rule was that school had to be held for one month to prove there were enough students to warrant a granting of the petition. Lorenzo Lyman volunteered the use of his home for the purpose. "Our home was turned upside down. There were 20 students, including the six children in our own family, crowding in our small house and you never saw such confusion. But the project was a success. One month later they started construction of Cloverdale School at the [southwest] corner of Ironwood and Judson Street [today's Perris Boulevard]. Next, the Armada post office was built on Alessandro at Judson," Rosa said.

Recalling her youth, Rosa described social activity that centered around the church and the community of Armada. "We used to have wonderful parties at the church—strawberry festivals, you know. Someone owned a cow and brought cream and others had berry patches and they were there for the picking. It didn't cost anyone anything. It was like one big family in the beginning here in the valley. There was wonderful spirit among them."

It was during the 1890 land rush that Rosa's future husband, William More, came to the valley from Redlands buying 10-acres on what is now Cottonwood Avenue between Perris Boulevard and Indian Street. In 1893, he built a house at 24685 Cottonwood Avenue. Bill brought his bride to the home when they married in 1898. Rosa described the valley's short-lived prosperity: "We had that life-giving water for only a few years, possibly five. Then the valley lost its water rights. After years of litigation, nearby towns won their claim of prior rights to the water which originated in the San Bernardino Mountains. When the water was withdrawn, the valley reverted to desert. Families left in droves, unable to make a living from the dry soil. One year, 35 houses were jacked up on rollers and hauled away by teams of horses. The beautiful vineyards and citrus groves disappeared. Fruit trees were cut up and used for firewood. The valley died." Settlers who stayed were stubbornly determined and hauled water from existing wells and springs. They put down wells where they could and held on.

The Mores had one child, Walter Lyman More, who was born in 1899 in the living room of their Cottonwood home "because the stairway to the upstairs was too narrow." Walter became a teamster in the early days for the Santa Fe Railroad as the company constructed the railroad through San Bernardino County and through Cajon Pass. Walter became a clerk in the Santa Fe Office in Riverside in 1917 and eventually became a vice president of the Santa Fe Railroad.

Rosa Lyman More passed away at age 98 on July 21, 1977. Her husband, William More, passed away in 1927. The couple is buried side-by-side at Olivewood Cemetery in Riverside. Their son, Walter Lyman More, passed away in 1983.

An Early History of the Law Firm of Best, Best & Krieger LLP

by John Brown et al

(Current Author's Note) - We hope that you will enjoy this most recent revision of a portion of the firm's "An Early History of Best Best & Krieger" first published in 1991 on the occasion of the firm's Centennial.

It is just what it says--the best account of our beginnings that we have been able to piece together. How the law firm of Best Best & Krieger LLP became Best Best and Krieger during its first 60 years. The firm has a rich history, marked especially by unique devotion to public service and community leadership. This is the kind of firm we have been, and still are, and we trust will continue to be.

An Early History of the Law Firm of Best, Best & Krieger LLP
BY
EUGENE BEST
ARTHUR L. LITTLEWORTH
DALLAS HOLMES
JOHN E. BROWN

Raymond Best, reading to become a lawyer with a law firm in Indiana in the late 1880's, began it all. Born on April 20, 1868 in Liberty Mills, Indiana, he graduated from DePauw University and became associated with the law firm of Frazer & Frasier in Warsaw, Indiana where he read law, apparently intending to become an attorney in Indiana. He moved to Riverside, California in March of 1891. The Riverside *Daily Press* noted on April 11, 1891 that "Raymond Best, a young law student from Warsaw, Indiana, who has been living in Riverside, has just passed a very credible examination at Los Angles and has been admitted to the bar." As was the custom in those days, Raymond's "examiners" were the then sitting members of the California Supreme Court who conducted a qualifying legal examination of Raymond at the Supreme Court's Courthouse in Los Angeles. After taking the train into Los Angeles from Riverside for his examination, Raymond was notified shortly after returning to Riverside that he had been admitted to practice law in California.

Before the year 1891 was through, newly-admitted attorney Raymond Best purchased the law library of John G. North, a lawyer and the son of the founder of the City of Riverside, John W. North. Best opened an office in the recently-built Evans Building, located in a rapidly urbanizing part of Riverside called the Evans Block. It was one of Riverside's first and certainly largest multi-story 19th Century office buildings. Raymond noted at the time that his Evans Building office was for the "occasional" practice of law. At that time there were 19 attorneys listed in

Raymond Best

John G. North (seated) and his secretary O. P. Saunders. After taking over North's practice, Raymond Best used this office for 62 years until his retirement in 1954 at the age of 85.

the Riverside City Directory, six listed in what would later become Riverside County towns and none in the Coachella Valley cities of Palm Springs or Indio. Raymond and his then law partner Oliver P. Widaman were called "able and reliable lawyers" and "a firm of prominent lawyers."

By the time Raymond Best moved to California, settled in Riverside, and was admitted to practice law, various efforts were afoot to form a dozen more new counties in Southern California, among them Riverside county. California had been admitted to statehood in 1850 and at that time Southern California included only three counties, Los Angeles, San Diego, and Santa Barbara. The new county of San Bernardino was added in 1853. By the time Orange County was formed in 1889, movements blossomed to form other new counties, particularly Riverside County, which was successfully formed in 1893. For the next 26 years the formation of Riverside County played a particularly important role in one of Raymond Best's most successful early business ventures.

The proponents of forming Riverside County advocated many arguments at the time for the formation of a new county. Some argued that San Bernardino was unfairly getting most of the credit for the small but increasing shipments of oranges from San Bernardino County. These amounted to 1600 carloads (railroad cars) in 1890 of which 1500 carloads, the proponents of the formation of Riverside County argued in 1891, were from Riverside alone. Also, the successful cultivation of the Washington Navel Orange and the attendant development of the City of Riverside, including the development of packing houses and other industrial uses servicing the cultivation of oranges, together with rapid development of commercial and residential uses, prompted rapid development and the continuing subdivision of and sales of real property in the City of Riverside for many decades to come.

The same year he settled in Riverside, Raymond Best founded his business, Riverside Abstract Company, in the City of Riverside. The abstract business was critically important to the buying and selling of land and as Raymond noted foundational to many of the later successes of his law firm. He noted years later that a title business would be more profitable than practicing law and ran that business by essentially putting his legal practice on hold. As Best himself acknowledged, he "practiced law as a sideline" for the next 27 years.

Raymond was the manager and controlling owner of Riverside Abstract Company (later Security Title Co. of Riverside and even later Safeco Title), from 1891 to 1917. Since an abstract of title summarizes everything that has happened with the title of a specific piece of property, it is critical to the buying and selling of land. It starts from the time the property was first recorded as owned and continues all the way to the present time, and the abstract was in those years a written instrument essential to both the seller and to the buyer as a fully-recorded history of what they were trading. As Raymond noted, preparing an abstract of title was much more laborious and expensive than preparing the title reports that became the norm much later in his career, in that it generally laid out at the time the entire history of a piece of property from the point that it was first recorded as an owned parcel of land. In one instance, Raymond remembered returning to his office with a brief case of abstracts tracing the chain of ownership of a piece of Riverside County property back to the King of Spain.

For the first couple of years Raymond Best managed Riverside Abstract Co., Riverside was part of San Bernardino County. Best remembered boarding the Santa Fe Railroad steam train in Downtown Riverside daily to ride to the San Bernardino County Courthouse to abstract the title records there and return them to Riverside. By the time Riverside County was formed he considered himself the most knowledgeable title and real estate attorney in Riverside County as that County established its own title records and title record keeping systems. More importantly, his research and his sale of abstracts of title familiarized him with buyers and sellers of land - bankers, developers, and speculators throughout Riverside County. Many of them became lifelong friends. In a 1954 news story, he told Riverside *Enterprise* Reporter Tom Patterson "Funny thing, I was known as an abstractor, not a lawyer." "While managing Riverside Abstract Co. Best constructed a separate building for that Company, which later housed the California Electric Power Company (Southern California Edison) on Eighth Street in Riverside.

Despite the demands of his new business, Best married Jennie D. Curtis on June 20, 1892 in Los Angeles, less than a year and one half after settling in Riverside. They were happily married for 65 years and had four children, daughters Rouie and Marie and his sons Eugene and Charles. The story of Best Best & Krieger would continue with that eldest. son, Eugene Best.

By the time Raymond resumed the fulltime practice of law in 1917, after selling Riverside Abstract Co., he had involved himself in civic and community affairs of the City of Riverside for nearly three decades. He and later his son, Eugene Best, were involved in civic affairs for decades in the City and County of Riverside, the State of California, and nationally. In addition to founding the Century Club, Best was a lifelong member of the Riverside Lions Club, having joined in 1924, was a member of the First Methodist Church of Riverside, and was President of the Riverside County Bar Association.

As a founder of and regular speaker to members of Riverside' Present Day Club, Raymond was an acclaimed public speaker known for his speeches to that club. The Riverside *Enterprise* noted on March 18, 1918, that "he has often spoken with eloquence on many of the live topics of day, always discussed there, indicating ability as a pleader of any cause he decides to espouse." In the subsequent May 31, 1918 Riverside *Enterprise* announcement of his candidacy for Riverside County District Attorney, he is called "one of the best public speakers in the county." The reporter also wrote, "He has a powerful voice and is most emphatic in his delivery." Best later advised his law partner John Gabbert that the ideal place to give an oration was a funeral, because the listeners were already in an emotional state. "At the 1915 funeral of Matthew Gage, the planner and developer of Riverside's Gage Canal," he told Gabbert, "I really had them going South!"

"Ray was a conservative Republican," said Gabbert, "but he subscribed to the New Republic for many years 'to keep an open mind.'" As chairman of the Republican County Central Committee in 1932, he was always proud of the fact that during the presidential election of that year, Riverside County was the only county west of the Mississippi that went Republican voting for Herbert Hoover as opposed to voting for Franklin D. Roosevelt. A highlight of Best's 86th birthday party in 1954 was Raymond reading a congratulatory birthday telegram from former President Hoover.

Although Ray Best was a lifelong pipe smoker, he was also a teetotaler and began the tradition of a dry law office for the firm, which lasted generations thereafter. At one luncheon at the Douglas Café under the Loring Opera House in Riverside, Gabbert remembers a few other lawyers and he ordering a beer on a hot day summer day. When the waitress asked Best whether he would like a beer, Best replied, "Yes, I would like one….in an icebox ten miles from here."

"Ray had a wonderful library, and was vulnerable to a good book salesman," said Gabbert. "He spent hours discussing law and law books, and in 1938 when I joined the firm we had the best law library around." Art Littleworth remembered that when he came to the firm in 1950, the collection of law books had long outgrown the library. Law reports for every state in the nation lined the hallways. Some books were never opened. Often there was room for only one person to squeeze through. Finally, there was no space at all, and some of the older leather bound volumes had to be moved to the unfinished attic of the Evans Building. That was usually a Saturday job for the young lawyers.

Best had two avid hobbies which he pursued in his large home on today's Mission Inn Avenue between Orange and Lemon Streets in downtown Riverside (where the Cheech Marin Center for Chicano Art & Culture now stands), and later at his and Mildred's home at 4542 Beacon Way. He was an ardent photographer, using glass plates and developing them in his own home darkroom. He also was an expert flower grower, specializing in dahlias and amaryllis. According to his partner John Gabbert, he spent much of his time toward the end of his career studying bulb catalogs and gardening publications from all over the world.

Raymond Best died on April 4, 1957 at the age of 88. On the occasion of his 86th birthday he noted, "There are several ways to achieve fame. The easiest one I practiced, is longevity." He also said in that same interview, "Well, Riverside has been pretty good to me in the way of giving me business. I've made very few enemies. I've always tried to be honest and square with everybody. I think I've established quite a reputation for integrity anyway."

Raymond Best's eldest son, Eugene, was born in 1893 and after graduation from Riverside Polytechnic High School in 1911, worked for his father's company, Riverside Abstract Co. He attended the University of Southern California and Stanford University. He obtained his engineering degree from Stanford as a Phi Beta Kappa in 1915, and then began to study law and abstract titles. He never attended law school, yet he took the bar examination in 1918 in much the same fashion his dad had 27 years earlier, passed, and was admitted to practice. The examination that year consisted of oral questioning by three appellate justices in Los Angeles, as well as a written examination of three questions which took about "one half hour to answer," according to Best. The entire matter was over in a day, he recalled. Late in the afternoon, the candidates called the clerk of the court who gave them their results, accepted their $2 library fee, and obtained their signatures on the oath to practice law. Gene returned to his position as escrow clerk at the Riverside Abstract Co. and much like his father got to know the lawyers, realtors, investors, and speculators involved in real estate throughout Southern California.

In the last months of World War I, Gene Best left Riverside to take up his duties as an instructor at the school of military aeronautics at Berkeley, California where student flyers received their ground work training. Best had enlisted for service in the Army and received his call to report for special duty at Berkeley. He was an instructor in mathematics and mechanics at the school. Mrs. Best and baby daughter Rouie followed him in a few weeks, and Berkeley would be their home during the time Mr. Best was stationed at the school. Following the war, Eugene and his family remained in San Jose where he did title work.

At Raymond's request, Gene Best soon returned to Riverside to assist his father in the practice of law. There were 31 practicing lawyers in the Riverside area. Before becoming a partner in the Best law firm in 1925, Gene Best opened an office in Lake Elsinore in 1923, which he operated on a one-day-a-week basis for over thirty years. Most importantly, Gene established, nearly 70 years prior to the more modern beginnings of his firm's present day municipal law practice, a municipal law practice for the Best law firm. He was appointed City Attorney of Elsinore in 1932, a position he occupied until 1954. From 1929 through 1940, he also served as City Attorney for the City of Riverside. Since the Best firm was appointed Lake Elsinore's contract city attorney in 1932, the firm has represented nearly 100 municipalities as contract city attorneys. That specialized legal practice all began with Gene Best, the City Attorney of Lake Elsinore and Riverside.

Gene was proud to become a named partner in the firm of Best & Best in 1925, but much like his father, had a variety of non-legal interests. Gene Best was an excellent machinist and woodworker, but his "number one skill and art was metal work," according to John Gabbert. He built still, stereopticon, and movie cameras and projectors, and even wrote an article for a popular science magazine on how to construct a movie camera. He played chess by mail on a national level, and subscribed to the Reader's

Eugene Best

Digest in Spanish in order to learn the language. He was a pilot and owned his own plane and after commuting by car to City Council meetings and office hours in the City of Lake Elsinore for 14 years vis-à-vis difficult roadways through the Temescal Canyon, began regularly flying his new Cessna airplane from Riverside to Lake Elsinore reporting that the trip from Riverside now consumed only seventeen minutes. He regularly piloted his own plane throughout the Western United States and to meetings of the Board of Governors of the California State Bar after being elected to represent Riverside, Orange, San Bernardino, and Inyo Counties in 1945.

During the second World War, he rode a scooter to work to save gasoline and worked after hours as a swing shift machinist at Hunter Engineering in Riverside to assist the war effort. Gene was a quiet, self-effacing man, but had an unusual capacity to analyze complex problems and reduce them to logical and understandable components. No one in town surpassed his reputation for professionalism and integrity, said Art Littleworth.

Best worked daily at the law firm's new offices at 4200 Orange Street through his early 80s. Art Littleworth said, "Even in those years, he could cut through the essence of the problem better than anyone else I've ever known." Years later, Gene Best was described in his obituary as "Diffident and unassuming." Best was an office lawyer who shied away from controversial cases. He stayed at work until his desk was clear. He had a quiet, analytical manner that helped build integrity and wide respect for the firm. James H. Krieger, another partner of Gene's, said "the rest of us are the workmen – he's the image." Art Littleworth said that when he joined the firm in 1950, "all you had to say was that you worked for Best's law firm and you were immediately welcomed anywhere in town." Eugene Best died in April of 1981.

For a time in the 1940's, the firm was known as Best, Best & Gabbert. John Gabbert attended schools in Riverside leaving only to finish high school at South Pasadena High School. John returned to Riverside to attend Riverside Junior College then went on to graduate from Occidental College, attended graduate school at Duke University, and graduated law school from the University of California's Boalt Hall (today known as Berkeley School of Law). He briefly entered private practice in Riverside and was appointed a Deputy District Attorney of Riverside County in 1935. In 1938, he joined Best and Best. The firm became Best, Best & Gabbert on July 1, 1941. After serving as a partner for two years and as a Riverside Police Judge, he enlisted in the United States Army in 1943. He returned to Best, Best & Gabbert in 1945 and resigned from the firm in 1949 when Governor Earl Warren appointed him as a Judge in the Superior Court of Riverside, a position he held from 1949 to 1970. At the time he became a Superior Court Judge his name was removed from the law firm's title. In May of 1970, Governor Ronald Reagan appointed him as Presiding Justice of the California Appellate Court, Fourth Appellate District, Division Two, a position which he held until his retirement in 1974.

James Krieger

Throughout his life, John Gabbert continued the Bests' commitment to civic affairs. He served as a school board member of the Riverside Unified School District from 1946 to 1949. He was president of the Riverside County Bar Association as well as the Lions Club, the Present Day Club, and the Citizen's University Club. He and other civic leaders advocated tirelessly for the University of California to establish a campus in Riverside.

Because of his long career as a lawyer, public official, judge and appellate justice as well as community leader, Gabbert very much set the tone for the rapid expansion of the law firm after World War II. With the help of a young lawyer named James H. Krieger who joined the firm three years before Gabbert left, the firm expanded rapidly. Krieger joined the firm in 1946 as an associate. He had also graduated from South Pasadena High School and attended Occidental College and the University of California, Berkeley. He graduated from Columbia Law School in New York City. He entered private practice in New York State but returned to California to join the law firm of O'Melveny & Myers in Los Angeles.

John Gabbert had known Krieger at South Pasadena High School and urged him to join Best, Best & Gabbert. In July of 1947, Krieger became a named partner in Best, Best, Gabbert & Krieger and when Gabbert left the firm to become a judge, the partnership became known as Best, Best & Krieger. The name of the firm has not changed since.

For the next 28 years, Jim Krieger built upon Gabbert's substantial water law practice, which began in the 1930's when Gabbert was the attorney for the Riverside Water Company and a number of other mutual water companies. Krieger specialized in water law and became one of the preeminent water lawyers in California and elsewhere by the time of his death in 1975. Krieger's water law practice led directly to the firm's representation of numerous special districts, school districts, cities, and counties and a variety of other public agencies, along with growing specialties in litigation, real estate, business, eminent domain bond counsel and natural resources law. That is how Best, Bests & Krieger became Best Best & Krieger LLP, today, 132 years later, one of the oldest and largest law firms in California.

Bibliography

Bar Bulletin of Riverside County.
Best, Best, and Krieger LLP. "Centennial History." Privately printed, Riverside, California: 1991.
Hemet *News*.
Lech, Steve. *Along the Old Roads*. Published by the Author, Riverside, California: 2004.
Los Angeles *Daily Journal*.
Press-Enterprise.
Riverside *Enterprise*.
Riverside *Press*.
Riverside *Daily Press*.

About the Authors

John Brown is a lawyer, Of Counsel to California's largest public law firm, and longtime historic preservationist. In his 48 year legal career with Best Best & Krieger LLP, he has served on his law firm's Executive Committee, was the firm's Marketing Partner for a decade and served as the firm's Municipal and Redevelopment Law Practice Group leader for 12 years. Brown's interest in historic preservation began with a law school planning internship to begin land marking the 1825 Russian Orthodox Church of the Holy Ascension in Unalaska, Alaska, now a National Historic Landmark. At Best Best & Krieger he was involved in the formation of the Mission Inn Foundation a non-profit formed to save the historic Mission Inn, a National Historic Landmark. He later served as the two term President of the Mission Inn Foundation where he headed up a "Bring it Home" campaign to collect lost, sold or stolen art, furniture and artifacts once housed in the 148 year old Mission Inn. In 2016 while serving as Vice President of the California Historical Society the City of San Francisco selected CHS as its lead partner to restore the Old US Mint by transforming that historic structure into a center of history, culture and learning.

Deanna La Cava grew up in Sunnymead, CA, today's Moreno Valley. She was the primary researcher providing the transcribed diary, photos and background material for the 36-part B. W. Tarwater Journal series that ran in the "Californian" newspaper in 1994. She wrote numerous articles on the local and natural history of southwest Riverside County for the same publication during the 1990s. In 1996, she won The Institute of History Award for Contributions to the History of San Diego from the San Diego Historical Society. Today, Deanna is Vice President of the Moreno Valley Historical Society and works steadily to get the story of the past in this city to the public.

Virginia Searl Sisk's great great grandparents on her mother's side were Dr. Isaac William and Emily Smith who settled at what is now Highland Springs in 1853. Her great grand father, James Marshall Gilman, settled in the Pass in 1869 near what would become the City of Banning. In 1871 James married Mattie Smith, daughter of Isaac and Emily. Documenting these ancestors and their histories has become a passion for Virginia. Born and raised in Hemet, her proximity to the Pass has been essential in her research of that area and its pioneers.

Subscribe to the

Riverside County Chronicles

Sign Up Now! The annual subscription is **$18** for two issues. These will be published in the Spring and Fall. To subscribe, just fill out the form below and return with a check made to:

Riverside County Heritage Association
P. O. Box 21168
Riverside, CA 92516-1168

- -

Subscription Form

Name: _____   Date: _____

Mailing Address: _____

_____

E-Mail Address: _____

Phone Number: _____

Please check the box if you want to be contacted about being one of our authors.   ☐

Made in the USA
Columbia, SC
26 June 2023